THE 2
INEVITABLE
INDELIBLE
INVIOLATE
INDOMITABLE
INGENIOU$
RULES OF
B2B MARKETING
W. WILLIAM HAINES

Most B2B market failures are not the result of poor tactics— they're the result of poorly applied marketing principles.

Here are 21 key rules that detail how to effectively leverage core principles for stronger marketing. Written for B2B marketers and business leaders, each rule can be read in 10 minutes or less. But don't read everything. You're busy. Just pick whatever topic is most relevant to you currently.

This book is short, on purpose
You're welcome

About the Author

Bill Haines has served as VP Marketing in very big B2B companies, in smaller ones, and even in start-ups. He's also been a principal at an award-winning mar-com agency and has spent a decade (and counting) consulting on business, product, and marketing strategy.
(Seems to have a bit of an attitude, as well.)

Why This Book?

> The carpenter grabbed his professional-grade power saw and cut the board to length. It didn't fit. Any other saw would have cut the board just as incorrectly. This was not a tool failure. It was a failure to apply a fundamental rule in carpentry:
>
> 'Measure twice, cut once.'

The latest marketing tools and approaches won't improve your B2B marketing unless you first assure that your fundamentals are sound. Take measure of your current approach. This book gives you a concise way to do so. So, do so.

The Leverage for More Effective B2B Marketing

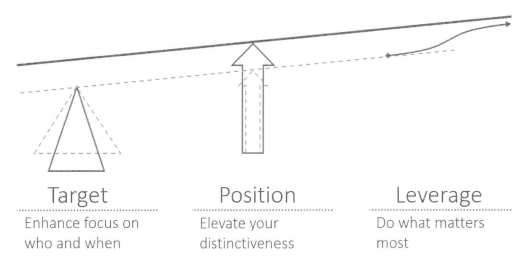

Target	Position	Leverage
Enhance focus on who and when	Elevate your distinctiveness	Do what matters most

Contents

No Forward, No Preface, No Dedication. See- right to the point.

Note to Reader

Don't read this book front to back.

Just flip through the pages to find a topic that's relevant to you right now and spend a few minutes on it. Each can be read in 10 minutes or less.

That's why I wrote it this way. So, don't screw-up my plan.

> *Look, you don't have time to read yet another 300-page, stultifyingly staid business book. Do you?*

Disagree with some things you find here? Typical Marketer.

Further note to the reader: This book is full of wry wit that is, at times, a bit acerbic. If you don't like wry wit, or you don't know what acerbic means, this book is not for you.

The Rules

0   Business books should not include filler content to make them longer

You are right- this is not actually a Rule. We're just using this as an example that shows how the book is set-up... in case you haven't already noticed.

WHY   For each rule we explain just WHY the rule is included.

For example, the "why" for this rule is that everyone is really, really busy- so you've got to get right to the point or you'll lose their interest. That goes for your B2B marketing too.

WHAT
- Concise bullet points give a top-line summary of just WHAT is covered in the topic
- If you are really attention-challenged, you can just scan this

HOW   Next, we describe HOW you can put the rule into practice. "How" seems pretty self-evident here. Just flip through the pages to see for yourself.

MORE   When we just can't say enough about a rule, here is MORE information to help you make sense of it. Also note the handy little table at the start of each Rule that illustrates just which of the 5- B2B Marketing Rule characteristics apply to the rule. (See: Glossary for an explanation of these terms)

And don't worry. There are 21 proper rules ahead.

NEXT

After every topic there is also a little space to jot your own notes about how you plan to take action on the topic. Use it. That's your point of reading the book, isn't it?

✓	Inevitable
✓	Indelible
✓	Inviolate
✓	Indomitable
✓	Ingenious

Read Time: 1 min.

Priority: 1

Complexity to Enact: Low

Target

Enhance focus on who and when

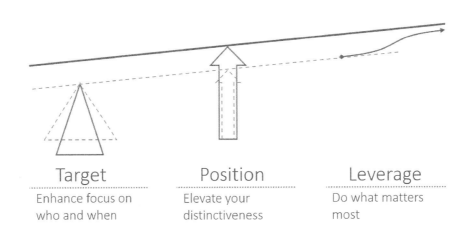

Target
Enhance focus on who and when

Position
Elevate your distinctiveness

Leverage
Do what matters most

1 Stop doing so many things, and focus

WHY

B2B marketing is about focus. So, while you can't be too dependent on any one tactic, you can't afford to dilute your efforts by using too many. There is no point in trying to do everything with a mile-wide, but an inch-deep approach. This only assures that everything you do will fail. You've got to focus on a few things that you can do really well.

By the same token, if your stable of tactics is too small, a failure in any one may be deadly. What if your assumptions were wrong about that singular route to market? What if it turns out that you can't get to every prospect in the same ingenious manner? What if the CEO asks you to describe your multi-channel marketing strategy?

WHAT

- Pick 4-5 market approaches and put 90% of your energy into these
- Create a "stop doing" list to eliminate the superfluous approaches so you can focus

HOW

Establish a manageable number of approaches. So, pick 4-5 market approaches to form the center of your strategy. These are the things you will pour 90% of your effort into.

Example- A Focused Set of Initiatives

1 We're going to institute an Account-Based Marketing program to increase revenue from our most lucrative customers.

2 We're going to create a speakers' bureau of thought leaders who can address the trends relevant to our product—then help them to get visibility via publications, social media, and conferences.

3 We're going to re-envision our sales enablement materials and practices by actually working with sales to build a program that's structured around the funnel.

✓ Inevitable
✓ Indelible
✓ Inviolate
Indomitable
Ingenious

Read Time: 3 min.

Priority: 1

Complexity to Enact: Low

Oops, that's only three—but you get the point.

Focusing your effort allows your chosen approaches to be effective— but you still need a small handful to assure that at least a couple will weather the market shifts that will inevitably come.

MORE
Be sure to consider all channel options, including the many digital options available, as part of a balanced approach. Still, that doesn't mean you should use them all.

"But isn't there more stuff I need to be doing?"

> "...Focus... means saying no to the hundred other good ideas that there are."
>
> Steve Jobs

Of course. You need to make sure you've got appropriate marketing automation tools in place; the right creative team and other resources; close relationships with Product, Sales, and Executives; the right venue for the holiday party...

Look, you already know all the general stuff you've got to attend to. Your calendar is chock-a-block booked with meetings about this stuff all day long.

The trick is to decide what among those things you are going to STOP DOING so you can focus (really focus) on that small handful of approaches that can yield big results in the marketplace.

So, close your door for 2 hours and make a list of all the things you and your team spend time on that are of dubious value. That's your "stop doing" list. Eliminating these things makes room for more focus on the few things that are really important to progress.

NEXT
What action can you take to try this for your business?

_____

2 Segment more carefully than you already have

WHY

"I already know my segments… are you kidding?"

Right—got it… No one enters a market or operates within one without already having a practical, real-world understanding of the segments they are serving. You do too. Heck, you've organized your product options and your marketing/sales efforts around your definition of segments.

So, clearly, we're not trying to fill an empty box here. The idea is to clarify attributes of your segments or identify sub-segments in order to improve the relevance of your messaging, your use of channels, focus of sales staff, and to discover new viable targets or eliminate wasted effort on poor-targets.

WHAT

- Dissect in order to reassess your segments
- Use appropriate B2B segment criteria to define segment alternatives
- Create a granular segment matrix to assess
- Then, consolidate similar segment threads to define just those that are clearly differentiated
- Prioritize segments using appropriate B2B criteria
- Involve others in the process for more complete insight

HOW

Overview As such, this process starts by organizing the understanding of your segments using a standard set of B2B **segmentation criteria.** This process can clarify the key factors that apply to each of those segments and illuminate segment organization, overlap, and gaps.

With clarified segments you next apply a set of **prioritization criteria** to rank the segments. We'll get to all this next.

Beware, this exercise requires focus, patient consideration, and a willingness to test your assumptions. But that's how you get to the next level. And that's what you want to do.

✓ Inevitable
✓ Indelible
✓ Inviolate
✓ Indomitable
  Ingenious

Read Time: 10 min.

Priority: 1

Complexity to Enact: High

About Traditional B2C Criteria

To be clear, B2C segmentation criteria are **NOT** what you'd use for a B2B business. To illustrate, B2C criteria usually look like this:

- Demographic
  - Age/ Gender/ Ethnicity/ Family
  - Education/ Income
- Geographic
  - Localized Regions
  - National/International
- Psychographic
  - Attitudes/ Values
  - Personality/ Lifestyle
- Behavioral
  - Purchase Triggers & Patterns
  - Benefits Sought

By contrast, B2B criteria are more... well... business-focused. On to the meat of it. There are 4 steps...

1 Create Segment Criteria Lists

Start by making lists for each of the following B2B segment criteria. You can later fine-tune this to the particulars of your business which will likely have characteristics that demand differences in your criteria. But in the meantime, build a base-line first by using these B2B segment criteria:

B2B Segment Criteria

Industries (the industries you serve or might serve)

Firmographic (Where do they work)
- Entity Types/Sizes (the categories of organizations within each industry broken down by size- S, M, L)

Domain (How do you get there)
- Regions (countries, regions, localities- as relevant)
- Channels (i.e. How prospects can be reached- e.g., distributors, particular sales regions/teams, direct channels, etc.)

Value Proposition (How can we uniquely satisfy their needs)
- Value Propositions that are relevant to the segment

Process (What purchase process do they use)
- Purchase Process (e.g., RFP process/ Quote/ e-Commerce, etc.- Scaled as: Heavy, Medium, Light)

B2B Segmentation Criteria
- Firmographic
- Domain
- Value Proposition
- Process

Example- Segment Criteria

Let's say you are a manufacturer of solvents that are used in several industries. First, pick one of the industries you serve. Let's take vehicle manufacturing as our example. Your list of segmentation criteria might look like this:

Industry: Vehicle manufacturers

Firmographic
- Consumer vehicle manufacturers- Large
- Commercial truck manufacturers- Large, Medium
- Construction machine manufacturers- Large, Medium
- Vehicle Restoration Firms- Small

Domain
- Regions
  - US based
  - Europe based
  - Asia based
- Channels
  - Direct sales
  - Distributor A
  - Distributor B

Value Proposition
- V1- Guaranteed just-in-time delivery
- V2- Harsh environment compatibility
- V3- Certified environmental standards compliance

Process
- RFP- Heavy weight
- Quote- Medium-Light weight
- e-Commerce- Light weight

Segmentation Criteria Provide a Framework for Thinking Through this Complex Issue

2 Create a Segment Criteria Matrix

Next, for each Industry you serve, or might serve, build a matrix with columns for each of the above criteria.

- Start each row with an Entity Type/ Size, then fill in each subsequent criteria column from left to right.

Example- Segment Matrix

Firmographic	Domain		Value Proposition	Process	
Entity Types	Region	Primary Channel	Core Value Proposition	Purch. Process Type	Purch. Process Weight
Consumer vehicle manufacturers- Large	US	Direct Sales	V1	RFP	Heavy
Consumer vehicle manufacturers- Large	Europe	Distributor A	V1	RFP	Heavy
Consumer vehicle manufacturers- Large	Asia	Distributor B	V1	RFP	Heavy
Commercial truck manufacturers- Large	US	Direct Sales	V2	RFP	Heavy
Commercial truck manufacturers- Medium	US	Distributor C	V2	Quote	Medium
Construction machine manufacturers- Large	US	Distributor D	V2	RFP	Medium
Construction machine manufacturers- Medium	US	Distributor D	V2	Quote	Medium
Vehicle restoration Firms- Small	US	Online	V1	e-Commerce	Light

Compare
+ Type
+ Region
+ Channel
+ Value Proposition
+ Process Factors

■ As you fill-in each associated column you may be defining a sub-segment. For example, Entity Type "Consumer vehicle manufacturers" are found in three regions: US, Europe, and Asia. Thus, each merit a separate "segment thread."

• Don't have any regional differences? Great. Leave that out…
• Or, perhaps, you just haven't yet explored regions that are different?

- Likewise, complete the Value Proposition, and Process columns.

With each row you are creating **Segment Threads.** These segment threads serve to deconstruct the key criteria that define market segments, so you assess the differences with clarity. When you do this with an extended team, the transparency of the criteria assures that everyone is discussing and debating the same things, instead of using the assumptions in their own minds. That's quite powerful because it prompts everyone to test their assumptions.

Obviously, the criteria you choose for your product/market will likely differ from this example. Yet you can leverage this framework using criteria that are appropriate to you.

And yes, the matrix gets quite long, frankly too long to be a useful list of market segments. But the thinking and discussion that goes into making it is invaluable in helping you to see things you may not have before. And worry not, the next step lets you make the list shorter again.

Deconstruct into segment threads to find important differences, then consolidate threads to form segments

3 Assess Segment Match

This is simply a matching game. You look at each of the segment threads you've constructed and identify those that can effectively be treated alike.

Example- Segment Matching

Construction machine manufacturers- Large	US	Distributor D	V2	RFP	Medium
Construction machine manufacturers- Medium	US	Distributor D	V2	Quote	Medium

In this example, taken from the prior example matrix of segment threads, construction machine manufacturers come in 'large' and 'medium' and have somewhat different purchase processes.

However, their common US regional location, common distributor channel ('D'), and the fact that their differing purchase processes are both medium weight and can be accommodated in a reasonably similar fashion, means that they can be combined into one segment.

═══════

To judge the match of segment threads, consider these questions:

1 Can the value proposition be the same or combined?
2 Can we get our message to them in the same or very similar manner?
3 Can we manage the sales process in the same or very similar manner?

B2B Prioritization Criteria
* Financial
* Psychographic
* Competitive
* Behavioral

If the answer to all three is "yes," they can probably be considered part of the same segment. If not, they likely must be treated as different segments. Now that was easy, right?

4 Apply Prioritization Criteria

Even after combining segment threads, you likely have a lot of segments defined. Thus, you now need to prioritize by applying a standard set of prioritization criteria that lets you score each segment and establish a rank order.

Like the segmentation criteria, you can later fine-tune this to the particulars of your business. But for now, build a base-line by using these B2B prioritization criteria:

B2B Prioritization Criteria
- Financial (see Glossary)
    - TAM (Total Available Market)
    - SAM (Serviceable Available Market)
    - SOM (Serviceable Obtainable Market)
    - Growth (Annualized Growth Rate)
    - ACP (Average Contract Price)
    - ACM (Average Contract Margin)
- Psychographic
    - Awareness (High, Medium, Low)

- Ability to Purchase (High, Medium, Low)
  - Competitive
    - Differentiation Strength (High, Medium, Low)
    - Competitors (A, B, C)
  - Behavioral
    - Competitor Vulnerability (High, Medium, Low)
    - Unmet Needs (High, Medium, Low)
    - Purchase Urgency (High, Medium, Low)

That's a lot of criteria, and in reality, you can't make good use of it all. So, **pick 1 or 2 from each category** and add them as columns to your matrix. Then rate each segment on each criterion using a 0-3 scale (0= lacks the attribute, 3= best.) Finally, add up the score for each segment to find the priority of each.

Weighting Criteria You may want to weight the criteria as well (e.g., You might give the "Avg. Contract Margin" and "Competitor Vulnerability" criteria each a 2x weight, making their portion of the overall priority score higher.)

"If you are not thinking segments, you're not thinking."
Theodore Levitt

Example- Prioritization

Firmographic	Prioritization Criteria					Score
	Financial		Psychographic	Competitive	Behavioral	
	3	1	1	1	2	
Entity Types	Serviceable Addressable Market	Avg. Contract Margin	Awareness	Differentiation	Competitor Vulnerability	
Consumer vehicle manufacturers- Large	3	1	3	2	2	19
Consumer vehicle manufacturers- Large	2	1	3	2	1	14
Consumer vehicle manufacturers- Large	3	1	3	2	1	17

Expand your segment matrix to include the Prioritization Criteria you have selected. Rate items on a 0-3 scale. Weight columns as needed and calculate total scores for each segment.

MORE   Make this exercise 10x more realistic by involving an
interdisciplinary team in the process.

The resulting discussion about the criteria, weighting and
scores will assure that all gain the insights of their peers and
improve their overall understanding of the segments. You'll
get smarter scoring of criteria. You will also create strong buy-
in for the results.

NEXT

What action can you take to try this for your business?

Jot a couple notes here:

_____

Segmentation
Goes Better
with Friends

_____

_____

_____

_____

_____

3 Refine personas around key B2B attributes, so your messages resonate

WHY

If you are not clear about the characteristics of the people whom you are trying to convince, you have little chance of saying something that is relevant, differentiated, and believable.

Personas are written descriptions of the types of people you wish to influence. B2B Personas include a specific range of factors that focus on the business nature of the person, rather than focusing on demographic attributes.

Understanding these attributes allows for the development of targeted messages suitable to the people who you wish to drive to action.

WHAT

- Construct core Personas that are based upon attributes that are particularly relevant in B2B markets
- Pay particular attention to B2B Buyer attributes
- Allow for continuous evolution of the Personas

HOW

Overview Perhaps you already have a set of personas that you use in your marketing efforts. If so, great. This section will offer a set of Persona Attributes appropriate for B2B markets that you could use to improve your existing Personas. If you do not yet have a robust set of Personas in place, these recommendations will get you going. Remember, you are focused on characterizing the business-related attributes of people here. While you should adapt the attributes to accommodate the particulars of your market, start with these:

B2B Persona Attributes

- Relevant Responsibilities & Activities/Workflows
- Needs/ Pains/ Gains
- Experience with Competitive Products
- Influence Profile
- Relevant Attitudes/ Background
- Exceptions

✓ Inevitable

✓ Indelible

✓ Inviolate

Indomitable

Ingenious

Read Time: 9 min.

Priority: 1

Complexity to Enact: Medium

B2B Persona Roles

Importantly, each Persona you describe will represent a person who fulfills one, or a combination, of three roles in relation to your product. Knowing the primary role of each Persona is critical to knowing how to message that Persona.

- **User** (Primarily a user of the product.)
- **Buyer** (Makes the financial decision to purchase.)
- **Influencer** (Exerts influence over others involved in the acceptance of your product. Can be internal to the target customer, or an external influence.)

Start With More Information Than You Need, Then Cut it Down

Any given Persona might fulfill more than one role. For example: A User of the product may also be its Buyer. Moreover, while some Personas can only be considered to be Influencers, (they neither use nor buy the product), all Users and Buyers also either exert influence or are influenced by others. Thus, the B2B persona framework described here incorporates an "Influence Profile" for all Personas. More on that later.

Let's start by detailing the core attributes of any Persona role you wish to define. Later we will address how these attributes should be modified in order to construct a Buyer Persona.

Keep in mind that, on average, 6-7 stakeholders are involved in a B2B sale. Your industry may differ. But suffice it to say that you will end up constructing several Personas in order to characterize each of the several different types of people who inhabit your various markets.

But, again, first the core attributes in detail.

Construct the Core B2B Persona

Below is a detailed description of the elements to include in your B2B Personas. Start by simply writing out the information for each attribute as succinctly as possible.

Persona Name

- Give the persona a memorable, common name. ['Bob' or 'Sally' are nice names.]

Role(s)

- User; Influencer; Buyer [Which one or combination of these apply? Which is the primary role?]

Job

- Typical Job Title [The most common title held by members of the persona group]

Relevant Responsibilities & Activities/Workflows

- Daily activities that potentially impinge on the product solution space. This can include job responsibilities, tasks done, workflows, etc. Anything the persona does related to your product space.
- Of particular interest for marketing use of the persona are the "triggers" (events or circumstances) which typically generate the product solution need.

Needs/ Pains/ Gains

- For any given Need (which can be thought of as a job to be done), there are usually factors that create Pains that the user wants relieved, and aspirational Gains that they would like to achieve.
- So, define the key things that the persona needs to get done and the related pain associated with the activity that needs a solution. In addition, if there are any larger goals related to the key things to be done, list those too.

Experience with Competitive Products

- List which products (or substitutes) the persona has used or is familiar with. 'Substitutes' are ways of meeting the need that don't involve your product or a competing product. These can be home-grown solutions, work-arounds, or even simply not addressing the need at all. Whether a competitive product or a substitute, you need to understand what you are competing with for the persona's interest.
- State how satisfied the persona typically is with their current solution.

Sometimes the 'competitor' is actually just the fact that the customer is willing to do without a solution at all

- Define whether the person's experience is current or past, and over what period of time. And if they typically are no longer using or considering competitive solutions- why?

Influence Profile

- All personas either exert influence over others or are influenced by others concerning your product space, or both. Detail this:
- **Influenced Via**: Where/how does the persona gain new information and viewpoints in their field, related to the solution space?
  - e.g., publications, websites, conferences & other events, associations, standards organizations, thought leaders, peers, staff, etc.
- **Exerts Influence**: In what way does the persona exert influence over potential buyers or users? Break this down as follows:
  - **Level**: [Champion; Influential; Communicator]
  - **Where**: [Within own company; External peer group; Industry-wide]
  - **How**: [Person to person; Social media; Publications or speaking; etc.]

Relevant Attitudes/ Background

- Here the primary concern is their predisposition regarding the acceptance/adoption of new solutions (e.g.,Early adopter, Pragmatist, Conservative) (Per the Chasm Model- See: Glossary)
- Also include any work or personal history that informs attitudes.

Exceptions

- Note any key variances

"Seems like an awful lot of stuff to include in a Persona if you ask me!"

Do you always whine this way? Look, just include the stuff that is relevant to your product/market space. In fact, you may think of additional characteristics that are vital to your space. If so, add those in. But if you are whinging because you don't know the answers to some of these things—well, perhaps you should. (See: Glossary for definition of "whinging")

Understand
the Persona's
Influence
Profile

- Influenced By?
- Influences How?

Example- Persona

Let's say you produce software that is used by R&D departments, sold on a SaaS model. This persona represents a type of key user of the software, one who strongly influences other users, the buyer, and who even contributes to the purchase decision-making process.

Bob

Role: User/ Influencer
Job: Research Team Manager
Relevant Responsibilities & Activities/Workflows

- Manages work assignments for team and oversees their work, prioritizes initiatives
- Responsible for productivity and overall success of group
- Manages department budget, including supplies utilization and costs
- Leads key research projects
- Key Triggers:
  - Assembling results data and financial measures for quarterly and annual reporting can be extremely time consuming and frustrating
  - Setting up new projects, (a few each quarter) is time consuming

Needs/ Pains/ Gains

- Need: Efficiently set-up new projects, track progress ongoing, and create compelling reports for management review
  - Pain: Routine paperwork, budgeting, and tracking are done using home-grown forms and spreadsheets that are hard to manage and don't give a consolidated view of all the needed information. There is a lot of manual entry.
  - Gain: Save time that can then be applied to work on the key research projects Bob loves to do.

Experience with Competitive Products

- Acme R&D Automation Systems- INSPIRE system
  - May have trialed the product within the last year but is typically rejected due to lack of flexibility to meet process/ workflow issues.
- Home-grown solution- Misc. forms, spreadsheets
  - Uses this approach currently, and it gets the job done at no additional cost (other than the extra time it requires of Bob)

"The aim of marketing is to know and understand the customer so well the product or service fits him and sells itself."
Peter Drucker

- Bob finds this frustrating, time consuming, and would like a better alternative

Influence Profile

- Influenced Via:
  - Peers at competing firms
  - Colleagues who have learned of valuable solutions from others
  - Attends scientific conferences, attends lectures, and typically compares products on the show floor
  - Reads scientific journals in his field
  - Subscribes to a couple scientific email newsletters/blogs, and reads periodically
- Exerts Influence:
  - **Level**: Can be a Champion-level influencer if he believes in the product
  - **Where**: Is quite influential with his company's buyer and often contributes actively to the buying process there. He also networks with peers at competing firms.
  - **How**: Typically involves person-to-person discussion with known others. Tends not to be active in posting via social media or other and is almost never a public speaker.

Relevant Attitudes/ Background

- As a researcher, he tends toward early adoption of new solutions, although he tends to want to test and evaluate options (he's a researcher!) Thus, his evaluation tends to be rather data-driven and objective.
- Typically, has worked at other companies with similar problems. So, this is a long-standing pain.

Exceptions

- None

Examine the Unique Attributes of Buyer Personas

Modifications for Buyer Personas

Unlike B2C markets, in B2B markets the Buyer is very often distinct and quite different from the user. If you don't know the buyer, understand the particular needs of the buyer, or reach the buyer with relevant messages, there will be no buying of your product despite how effective your product may be for users.

B2B Buyers typically take the recommendation of lead users concerning which of the available product options will best meet their needs. However, Buyers have their own needs that must be met. These often center around contract terms, service, warranty, financing, price, bundled offerings, discounts, delivery, vendor stability, productivity impacts, training, customization/ adaptation process and rights, integration with other products, and other factors. Practical stuff. Buyers typically try to take-into-account the total business impact of the purchase, not just the impact on the user or on a particular outcome.

So, this makes the Buyer a complex target that requires the spelling-out of some additional factors. To flush-out a Buyer Persona, start with the Core B2B Persona framework, then modify it as follows:

Revisit and Improve Personas as you Learn More Over Time

"Relevant Responsibilities & Activities/Workflows"
- "Daily activities that potentially impinge on the product solution space or product users."
  For Buyers, cover the following:
  - Product evaluation/ consultation
  - Negotiation & Contracting process
  - Approval process

"Needs/ Pains/ Gains"
For Buyers, determine which of the following are particular areas of concern to the Buyer, and add information:
- Product 'Credence' factors that are important, e.g.,
  - Validation that the Product satisfies user needs
  - Productivity impacts due to Product adoption
- Product Support factors that are important, e.g.,
  - Vendor stability
  - Warranty
  - Service/ Customer Service/ Technical Support
- Financial factors that are important, e.g.,
  - Price
  - Volume-based or other Discounts
  - Bundled offerings (e.g.: multi-product purchase deals)
  - Payment terms/ Financing
- Implementation factors that are important, e.g.
  - Delivery

- Training
- Customization/adaptation process and rights
- Integration with other products

"Experience with Competitive Products"

For Buyers, who may not have direct experience with competitive products, determine what they understand:

- Understanding of the user's product experience
- Understanding of the overall company experience with the competitor- including the factors listed under "Needs/Pains/Gains" above

MORE All of this would seem to be ambitious enough, wouldn't it? It's a lot of work to construct a full set of personas. So, start with the most important one and work to fine tune your version of the framework, accommodating the realities of your market. Then build others in priority order.

Same Page Personas are also commonly a key element of product development work. Establishing Personas that are shared and evolved by both product and marketing staff can help assure that everyone is on the same page.

Not Too Fancy Many companies turn Personas into fancy documents with a high level of design. But keep in mind that Personas are usually internal, working documents that should be readily modified whenever your understanding of the people in your market change. Don't slow that process by insisting on making them too pretty.

What Changed When you revise Personas, flag the specific changes you make and explain why it changed. In this way, those who have relied on the prior version of the Persona will be able to readily understand why the target has moved and will be better able to adapt to the change.

NEXT

What action can you take to try this for your business?

4   Map the customer's journey to understand when and how you can exert influence

WHY

It's just not as simple as: send an email, get an order.

B2B sales result from multiple contacts and the nurturing of prospects from their first recognition of a need through to their adoption and reordering or referral of your product. If you don't know in what stage of the process the prospect is currently, you don't know what to say that will be relevant and compelling. If you don't know how to reach the prospect at that stage, you can't.

Note This is **NOT** the map of your customer's experience with your product, (though that should be a part of it). This is broader- because we're talking about both acquiring and keeping the customer. Acquisition starts before they touch your product.

So, you must map things out in detail.

WHAT

- Outline the customer's journey for each Market and Persona from Awareness through Experience
- Define the key customer events within each phase
- Specify the activities, success criteria, and emotional status of customers within each event
- Define the objectives, key touch-points and influence opportunities you have within each event
- Build the map in matrix form for easy updating, and revisit it regularly

HOW

Yes, your particular customer journey will be unique to your market and your product. But you can use a core B2B marketing framework to flush-out that journey as follows:

Use a spreadsheet to build this. On the horizontal (time) axis list the core phases of the journey:

✓	Inevitable
✓	Indelible
✓	Inviolate
	Indomitable
✓	Ingenious

Read Time: 5 min.

Priority: 1

Complexity to Enact: High

- Awareness (Demand Management)
- Consideration (Lead Management)
- Decision (Opportunity Management)
- Experience (Loyalty Management)

Columns Under each phase, set-up columns to represent the **key events** that take place within each phase, (e.g., within the Awareness phase the prospect likely first has a "Realization of Need", then goes through a "Need Clarification" step.)

Rows Use rows in the matrix to represent the important stuff related to each "Key Event", including:

- **Activities** that prospects typically carry out during the event
- The Prospect's **success criteria** for the event
- Your **objectives** during the event (i.e.: What you want to achieve with the prospect during that event)
- How prospects typically **feel** at this point
- **Touch-points** you potentially have with the prospect during the event
- Ways you can exert **influence** at these touch-points to achieve your objectives

Use a Cross-Disciplinary Team to Think Through the Details of the Map

Leverage Perspectives The above will give you a useful framework to think it all through. Put together a cross-functional team to work on this (marketing, sales, product, and anyone who has intimate knowledge of the customer.)

- Discuss the key 'events' that they see in the real world of customers. Gain perspective on what really happens during those events, to whom, why, and the impact.
- Most of what you need to know is the minds of those around you. Gather these insights and distill them into a common understanding of the journey.
- Where your knowledge is still lacking, go visit customers and observe.

In the end, if you don't come away with a much better understanding of the customer journey, you're not doing this right. Try again.

Example- Journey Map Framework

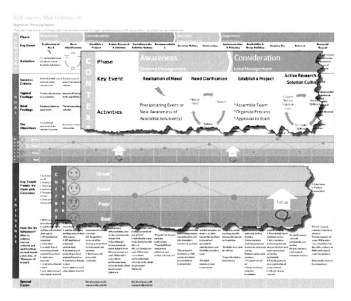

There is no, single 'right' way to do a journey map

Journey maps don't need to be fancy. The one pictured here is fairly straight-forward. Yours will look different. The journey map just needs to document the key stages that the customer goes through, so you know what to do with them.

Since this picture is impossible to read, you may want to download the template to get yours started: **21b2bRules.com**

Different Strokes The customer journey map for different Segments and Personas are going to be different. So, you're going to have to build a map for each one that differs. Yes, yes—B2B marketing is hard. Get over it.

Bottom line, there is no, single correct way to configure a journey map. There are an almost unlimited number of reasonable approaches, and this makes getting started a problem for most marketers. So, use this as your framework to get started.

MORE

Living Document As with segmentation, Personas, and many other tools of marketing, your journey map should be a living document. Revisit it whenever something changes in your market or you uncover additional insights. And like those other tools, this should be shared and contributed to by the broader interdisciplinary team at your company. That kind of collaboration and transparency keeps everyone on the same page and assures that all the decisions about managing prospects/ customers stem from a common vision.

Make It Work The journey maps you create will be unique to your market/ product and should communicate in a manner that is meaningful to you, your team, and the broader organization. The framework offered here is just that- a framework. Use it to improve journey maps you already have or as the start of new ones. Regardless, use your own insight to make it better. That's why they need you.

Regularly
refresh your
journey maps

NEXT

What action can you take to try this for your business?

Jot a couple notes here:

_____

_____

_____

_____

5   Know how your product impacts your customer's customer

WHY

Your B2B customer cares more about their customer than they care about you.

Understanding your customer's goals for their own customers will allow you to better align what you say about your benefits. In essence, your benefits must support the benefits they offer to their customers.

WHAT

- Learn your customer's customer
- Create a benefit chain matrix to align your value to how your customers convey value to their customers

HOW

This comes down to a matter of understanding what is downstream from your customer and of thinking clearly about this as you formulate your own value proposition.

Know Who Their Customers Are

You learn this by asking simple questions. You can do research yourself, talk to your sales team, or better yet, have a direct conversation with your customers.

- Do your customers have direct customers? Who are those customers? List and categorize them. Utilize the market segments that your customers use for their customers.
- Do your customers work through distributors, channel partners, or others who they must satisfy? Again, categorize these.

Know Their Benefits

For each of the above categories of your customer's-customers, catalog the key benefits that your customers promote to them.

First determine what key benefits they message to each of their customer categories.

✓ Inevitable
✓ Indelible
✓ Inviolate
✓ Indomitable
✓ Ingenious

Read Time: 3 min.

Priority: 2

Complexity to Enact: Low

Next, identify how your benefits support your customer's messaging to its customers. Detail this benefit chain using a chart:

Benefit Chain

Your Customer's Customer Categories	Key Benefits Your Customers Promote to Their Customers	Our Benefits that Align to Their Benefits
Category 1	Their Benefit A Their Benefit B	Our Benefit X
Category 2	Their Benefit A Their Benefit B Their Benefit C	Our Benefit X Our Benefit Y
Category 3	Their Benefit B Their Benefit C	Our Benefit Y

It's simple, but by methodically mapping your customer's-customer categories and what your customer says to those targets, you have a framework that you can use to better align your own messages to what they believe makes them successful.

In turn, you can then speak directly to how your product supports their message. It's not rocket science, but it does require some discovery and clear thinking.
(See Also Rule: Get the value proposition perfectly on target before you put effort into tactics.)

MORE

Obviously, this does not apply to every B2B product or market. In truth, this is really just an extension of understanding your customer. But sometimes we become so focused on our own product's benefits that we forget the larger purpose those benefits serve for customers.

Don't expect your customers to make this intellectual leap on their own. Make it explicit for them.

NEXT

What action can you take to try this for your business?

_____

_____

_____

Your Customer's
Customer is Your
Concern Too

_____

_____

_____

_____

Position

Elevate your distinctiveness

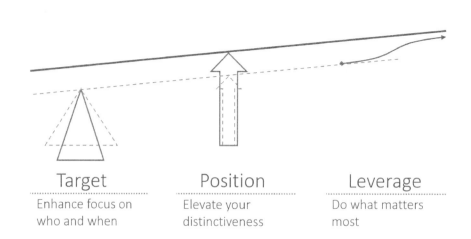

Target	Position	Leverage
Enhance focus on who and when	Elevate your distinctiveness	Do what matters most

6 SWOT more strategically to find competitor vulnerabilities

WHY
Yes, you are already doing "SWOT". But the real value in this long-standing exercise comes when it is used as a framework to understand how those Strengths, Weaknesses, Opportunities, and Threats signal vulnerabilities in your competitors.

WHAT
- Do a traditional SWOT
- Determine strategies at the intersections of S/W – O/T
- Complete this for your company and competitors, then compare to refine your strategy

HOW
Overview To SWOT strategically, first define the key Strengths, Weaknesses, Opportunities and Threats that exist for the company or product (just as you've done previously).

But then take it a step further by developing strategies to:
- Leverage strengths against opportunities and threats
- Mitigate weaknesses against those same opportunities and threats.

A handy matrix follows.

✓ Inevitable
✓ Indelible
✓ Inviolate
✓ Indomitable
  Ingenious

Read Time: 4 min.

Priority: 1

Complexity to Enact: Medium

Strategic SWOT Analysis

Here is the matrix you use to build this more strategic version of SWOT analysis. First, complete the top & left boxes of the matrix.

Ask Both What We Can Do, and What They Can Do

	List External Opportunities for the company or product here	List External Threats of the company or product here ... ...
List Key Strengths of the company or product here	Strategy: How can the company/ product leverage its inherent Strengths to take greatest advantage of these Opportunities.	Strategy: How can the company/ product leverage its inherent Strengths to diminish the impact of these Threats.
List Key Weaknesses of the company or product here	Strategy: How can the company/ product minimize its inherent Weaknesses by using these Opportunities.	Strategy: How can the company/ product minimize its inherent Weaknesses to avoid these Threats.

With the standard SWOT information filled in, it's time for the hardest, but most valuable, part- completing the 4 inside boxes. Think through the strategy questions in the matrix.

Do this first for your own company or product, then do it for each of your 1 or 2 key competitors. Doing this kind of SWOT on your competitor can uncover the types of actions they may be likely to make, and the vulnerabilities they have.

You are thinking inside their heads.

"But what if I don't know much about the competition?"
It certainly can be difficult to find information. Often, it's difficult just to actually take a look at the competitor's product. If so, it may be time to leverage the thought leaders and analysts you know, customer panels you have, or to

reach-out to the competitor's customers. This can be tricky because you don't want them to reveal proprietary information. So, your questions might focus on their impressions and on what disappoints or delights them about the competitor's product. You can use a variety of questions to probe around this, such as: "How did things go before the competitor's product compared to after? Why? What was the business impact? How are things changing? What's next?" Etc. From there you have to make inferences.

Comparative SWOT

Finally, compare the Strategic SWOT you did for your company or product to that which you did for a competitor. Consider a few questions as you do. Your answers will form the basis of your strategy against that competitor.

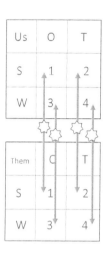

- How do your strategies compare to what you think theirs might be? (e.g., potential market impact; how viable is it to pull-off)
- What changes to your strategies might help to circumvent theirs? (It's a bit of a chess game—prevent the opponent from getting an advantage.)
- Is there a key vulnerability that you could exploit? (did you have an "ah-ha" moment?)

MORE   As with most of our B2B marketing rules, leveraging people who have different perspectives can help to make this exercise more insightful and valuable. In addition to representing different internal perspectives, consider including outsiders in this effort, such as thought leaders or customers.

NEXT

What action can you take to try this for your business?

Jot a couple ideas here:

"Even if you
are on the
right track,
you'll get run
over if you just
sit there."

Will Rogers

_____

_____

_____

_____

_____

_____

_____

_____

7 To differentiate, dissect the full product ecosystem, not just product features

WHY

Your product must be differentiated to be considered. Otherwise, you are an "also ran", and are easily dismissed.

Fortunately, differentiation does not only come from the product's features. The full "ecosystem" that you wrap around your product can be the greatest differentiator. In fact, things like support, warranty, and ease of acquisition can be very strong differentiators expressly because such things can be particularly important to B2B customers.

🕐 Read Time: 4 min.

WHAT

- To differentiate, consider all factors including product benefits, product attributes, and the broader product ecosystem you (could) offer
- Brainstorm with a team, then validate insights with customers

Priority: 2

HOW

Think About Three Tiers of Your Offering

ⓘ Complexity to Enact: Medium

Product Benefits We're always supposed to lead with the benefits, right? Right. Benefits describe how your solution gets rid of customer pain and/or fulfills their aspirations. Yes, you must get this right, and ideally this is where you find your greatest differentiation. But what if you don't?

Product Attributes More commonly referred to as features. You do the comparative feature grid to show how your offering stands up against competitors. You highlight the relative value of your features over that of your competitors. You differentiate your feature set to the greatest degree you can. Yet, still, perhaps in order to satisfy the core benefit needs of customers your feature set must be pretty much the same as everyone else's. And thus, the prospect will look at your features and still end up saying: "eh".

Product Ecosystem In B2B, there are frequently customer needs that exist outside the normal realm of features and benefits. Sometimes these are unrecognized by the prospect ("latent"). Many times, they are the kinds of things that are particularly attractive to buyers, though uninspiring to users. These are things like:

- Financing/ payment terms
- Bundling options
- Delivery terms/ logistical support
- Warranty/ guarantee
- Implementation/ integration/ technical assistance
- Customer service
- Maintenance
- Training
- Custom modifications
- Process or engineering support
- Others…

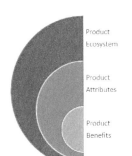

Product
Ecosystem

Product
Attributes

Product
Benefits

Importantly, these factors can be very differentiating.

So, think through these product ecosystem possibilities from the outset. Pay particular attention when you have an existing product that is not well differentiated and which you can't change substantially. In fact, think this through even if you can. The blanket that "wraps around" your product may give buyers just the differentiation that makes them stand up and not say: "eh", but instead say: "hey!"

OK—so no doubt you already surround your offering with at least some of these. Wonderful. You are thinking smartly. But could you refine or expand what you're doing? Could you use this category of stuff to further differentiate? Regardless of what you can or can't do with the product-proper, could you find another latent buyer need to satisfy with your product ecosystem? Or, at least, could you expand, clarify, or simplify what you are already doing?

Alternatively, perhaps there is something in your ecosystem that you could stop doing (like having exceedingly complex contract terms)? Yes, think it through.

Of course, these are all things that require the involvement and buy-in of others within your company. But, someone must start the ball rolling by identifying what can make the product more differentiated and marketable. You?

MORE   On balance, it is your full and complete solution offering that you must differentiate. So, do the following to pin it down:

1   Pull together a small, interdisciplinary team- Marketing, Product, Sales, CS, Finance- people who have some perspective to offer. Schedule a 2-hour ideation session.

2   Whiteboard each of the three tiers. Start with Benefits, then move to Attributes. Brainstorm what else could further differentiate your offering. Then, when the conversation turns to laundry-listing all the reasons that you can't implement changes to these things, switch to discussing the product ecosystem. This can be a more free-ranging discussion. Use your buyer personas as a guide.

Brainstorm to Identify Potential Product Ecosystem Value

3   The output of the session is a list of potentially differentiated product ecosystem value generators that you can then validate with buyers. Yes, customer discussions follow. Those discussions will both clarify what is and is not valuable and will also lead to further ideas.

Importantly, such customer discussions may be set-up by sales but should not include them. This discussion is not about selling what you have. It's about solving problems that haven't come to your attention before. You don't want to cloud the customer's feedback with the looming prospect of a sales pitch.

NEXT
What action can you take to try this for your business?
Jot a couple notes here:

_____

_____

"Every
business is a
service
business."

Philip Kotler

_____

_____

_____

_____

_____

_____

8   Define your Positioning Platform simply and visually

WHY

Like time, your differentiation is relative. But to what?

"Positioning" reflects the way your product delivers value to customers that is different from that of competitors. It's the center-point of what you will say to the market, as well as the hub around which you will build your key market messages.

As such, your positioning must be expressed clearly and understandably so that everyone within your company gets it and can build on it. Doing so both in words and in visuals makes your positioning explicit enough to be the rallying point it needs to be.

WHAT

- Complete a traditional positioning statement
- Create a diagram to express how your product compares to competitors on the two, most important attributes
- If possible, use quantified data to structure the diagram

HOW

The Positioning Statement

Having dissected the full product ecosystem to find your differentiation from your competition, (See Rule: To differentiate, dissect the full product ecosystem, not just product features) you will want to synthesize this into a positioning statement. We've all done these. They follow the format:

For [your target] who [state their need or want], [your product name] is a [the product's category] that [the product's compelling benefits]. Unlike [your key competitor] [your product] [statement of its key differentiation].

Make sure that you have written such a statement. As an internal document, it doesn't have to be pretty, but it does have to be very clear. So, don't worry too much about how

Inevitable

Indelible

✓ Inviolate

✓ Indomitable

✓ Ingenious

Read Time: 4 min.

Priority: 2

Complexity to Enact: Low

melodious the words sound. Get the idea of it right and express it in unmistakable terms.

A companion to the positioning statement is the **positioning diagram**. This is a visual depiction of your product's distinctive position relative to that of the competition. It allows your stakeholders to literally see what you're talking about and can be the very thing to elicit the "ah ha!" moment that sparks the buy-in and support of skeptics.

The Positioning Diagram

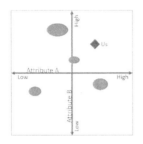

Pick 2 Key Product Attributes
To build your positioning diagram, start by picking 2 key measures of differentiation that you have discovered, e.g., cost, ease of use, integration, performance, ROI, quality, security, service, etc. (These are general examples. Obviously, you want to use whatever attributes are really key to your market and part of your core differentiation.)

Rate Competitors
Pick your 2 most important competitors and rate each on these two product attributes (scale 1-10).

Likewise, rate your product.

Set-up the Diagram
Put one product attribute on the X axis and the other on the Y axis

Plot
Plot your product and the competitor products on the quadrant diagram based upon the scores you've assigned.

Do you overlap with competitors? If so, identify alternative key attributes where you don't. If you can't come up with any, revisit the prior rule (See Rule: To differentiate, dissect the full product ecosystem, not just product features)

You need distinctiveness that matters to your market.

If you wish to make the diagrams even more descriptive you can size the competitor circles in proportion to their relative market share, number of customers, revenue, or another metric. Anything to get your point across visually.

The key point here is that the diagram illustrates the reasoning behind your positioning statement. In fact, creating the diagram is a great help in formulating the positioning statement to begin with, particularly if you are working with a team to develop it, (as you should.)

Together, these elements form your **Positioning Platform**.

MORE

Are the scores you use in the diagram objectively quantifiable? You can leverage market data that you already possess, that you purchase, or that you gain through your own research to quantify the values used. This can be as simple as having prospects score both your product and competitors on the attributes you have selected. Whichever way you acquire data, when that data is used to create the diagram it gives it a higher level of credibility within your organization.

Quantify the Diagram Axes if Possible

But don't let the absence of such data deter you from creating a diagram based upon your assumptions. This will help you to clarify your assumptions, and thus do a better job of validation.

"Should I present this diagram within marketing materials?"

Maybe. Use this primarily as an internal document that will help stakeholders (the creatives, sales, product development, executives, etc.) to understand the position. But for your market it may be just the kind of visual representation (after prettying it up) that will communicate well to them. Your decision.

NEXT
What action can you take to try this for your business?

_____

_____

"Positioning is
not what you
do to a
product.
Positioning is
what you do to
the mind of
the prospect."

Al Ries

_____

_____

_____

_____

_____

9 Perfect your value proposition before you put effort into tactics

WHY
Most market failures don't result from poor marketing tactics. They result from going to the market with a poor marketing message, i.e.: not Relevant, Differentiated, or Credible to the target market.

No matter how strong your marketing database, creative, and tactical approaches may be, if you aren't saying the right things to the right people at the right time, your efforts will fail to produce the level of results you want.

WHAT
- Create the core messaging deck
- From this, build the core value proposition
- Then create market and persona-specific versions

HOW
Value Proposition and Messaging are how you communicate your reason to buy to customers. They stem from your Positioning. Recall that your Positioning Platform is an internal document that describes the way your product delivers value to customers that is different from that of competitors. If you haven't already, get your Positioning Platform together first. (See Rule: Define your Positioning Platform simply and visually)

Overview With your Positioning Platform in hand, you first build a set of Benefit Messages, then derive the Core (cross-segment/ cross-persona) Value Proposition from them. Later you can create segment-specific and/or Persona-specific versions that are based the Core.

First, we'll focus just on the Core.

Create the Core Messaging Deck
This consists of a set of statements that each describe a particular benefit and how that benefit is special or unique. Messages should first be written as an internal document but will later be converted into marketing copy for use in

✓	Inevitable
	Indelible
✓	Inviolate
✓	Indomitable
	Ingenious

 Read Time: 6 min.

 Priority: 1

 Complexity to Enact: Medium

promotional materials. (Example provided below.) **What follows offers an approach to creating messages.**

Hear the VOC When messaging fails to impact the customer it is almost always because the company has made false assumptions about what is truly of value to those customers. To get your message right you've got to talk to customers, (hear the Voice-Of-Customer.) That does not mean reading reports from sales (who, you may have noticed, have their own perspective). You must also hear this yourself directly or through objective intermediaries (e.g., researchers).

Message Criteria
* Relevant
* Differentiated
* Credible

It's useful to start with your assumptions about what the benefits are, then use your market feedback to validate (or change) those assumptions. When you talk to customers, a **key question** to ask is: What would you tell anyone who offers this kind of product that they should or should not do in order to improve their success with you? Keep it that open-ended. You'll get all kinds of answers you might not expect.

You want your Benefit Messages to express your solution to the real-world needs, pains, and desired gains of target customers; address their experiences with competitive solutions; and embody their attitudes about the value of a better solution. (We're back to building understanding about the Personas who you are courting.)
(See Rule: Refine personas around key B2B attributes, so your messages resonate)

Message Structure Messages can be written in any form that clearly and succinctly puts the point across. Here's a standard format you may wish to use:

[State the specific benefit created] by [State the special or unique approach]

Example

"Uses proprietary RFID capture to simplify and speed data collection in the field."

▬▬▬▬▬▬▬▬▬▬

Remember that benefits may be derived from the greater product ecosystem as well. You might consider clustering more than one such benefit into a message.
(See Rule: To differentiate, dissect the full product ecosystem, not just product features.)

Brainstorm It's valuable to hold a brainstorm session with colleagues to test your assumptions and to create an expanded list of message candidates. The discussion you have will yield a long list of potential messages that should each hang off the intersection between customer needs and your solution. Great!

Some of these will be specific to a particular market or persona. That's fine. Some will be more general in their appeal. Wonderful. Some of the specific ones can be revised to give them more cross segment/ Persona appeal. Do so, (but keep the originals too.)

Now **rank** the list of general-appeal messages and dress-up the best ones a bit. Here is the acid test. Ask: Is this message fully compatible with our overall Positioning? If not, you know what to do. If so, terrific. You want 6-8 of these messages. This is your Core Messaging Deck.

Supporting Evidence Just one more thing: For each message, 1 or 2 pieces of supporting evidence should be provided that defend its statement of benefit. The source of this evidence can be surveys or other studies, testimonials, adoption statistics, thought leader opinion, etc. This supporting evidence will likely be utilized in your marketing materials as, well, support for the benefit statements you make.

Leverage the Messaging Deck to brief the creative team, and as a content source for development of collateral material

---

Example
"We saw a 40% decrease in the amount of time needed to capture data in the field."
P. Govindan, General Manager, Acme Industrial

Create the Core Value Proposition

With 6-8 core messages in hand, you are ready to construct the Core Value Proposition. This is a customer-facing statement that can be used in promotional materials. It must be expressed in the customer's language, (i.e., no jargon or hyperbole) and must succinctly convey how the product is uniquely valuable to the prospect.

To attack building the Value Proposition it's helpful to first organize your benefit messages into master-subordinate relationships. (Some benefits are actually sub-parts of a broader benefit or might support it in some way.) You may find that your Core Value Proposition is creating itself through this exercise. In any case, the Value Proposition structure you're going for looks like this:

> Lead Line State the product's overarching, special benefit in an attention-getting way. There's no set format here, but it should express the idea within 3 seconds.
>
> Clarifying Statement Describe how that benefit is delivered to target customers that makes it particularly valuable.
>
> Supporting Points List subordinate benefits. Prepare 3 of your key messages in customer-facing language to use here.

Express your value proposition in the customer's voice

Example

Lead Line: "Reduces cost and errors so you can focus on customer service instead of customer complaints."

Clarifying Statement: Our mobile management solution simplifies your staff's data collection, manipulation, and reporting where they need it most- in the field.

Supporting Points:
- "Simplifies and speeds data collection in the field using RFID capture."
- "Seamless integration with your existing CRM."
- "Eliminates the most common data input errors."

Solidifying the Value Proposition requires rounds and rounds of revision. Of course, you should get market feedback on the rounds you feel good about- so you can then feel less good about them- and make them better. We've given you the structure, but the magic belongs to you.

You may need segment and persona-specific messaging

Create Segment/Persona Specific Versions

With the core Value Proposition established, you can go to town creating versions of it that speak more directly to specific Market Segments or to specific Personas. This may only require adjustments to the Supporting Points that you attach to the Lead Line and Clarifying Statement. However, you can change anything as needed as long as your Segment or Persona-specific Value Proposition is compatible with your Core Value Proposition.

MORE Throughout this process you must focus on who it is you are speaking to. What is important to them? What kind of language do they normally use? What are the other guys saying?

Remember, your Value Proposition must exhibit the same characteristics as your messaging: relevant, differentiated, credible.

NEXT

What action can you take to try this for your business?

Jot a couple notes here:

"The reason it seems that price is all your customers care about is that you haven't given them anything else to care about."

Seth Godin

10 Remember, B2B customers are people too

WHY B2B prospects/customers can be just as emotionally and personally driven as B2C consumers. The customer is not just a shapeless, corporate entity. It is some human being, or group of humans (yes, even purchasing managers are humans), who are every bit as subject to human needs, fears, impulses, and errors as are B2C consumers.

Good thing. It gives you something human to hook into with your marketing efforts. But only if you really understand your prospect as a human.

WHAT
- Consider the human elements of B2B customers- their more personal side and mindset, and demonstrate your understanding of this
- Use this understanding to build trust- the factor that overcomes many other obstacles

HOW First, act on the Rule: *Refine personas around key B2B attributes, so your messages resonate.*

Tell Me Where It Hurts The question is: What kinds of human issues get under the prospect's skin? -- Are they risk-averse? Do they desperately want to appear expert? Do they gain respect by finding the most innovative solution or by securing the most proven alternative? What kinds of pressures are they under? How can purchase of your product improve their job satisfaction, enhance their prestige, reduce anxiety, etc.?

Psych B2B marketers often make the mistake of assuming that the purchase decision will be made almost entirely based upon rational factors. It will not. It will be a combination of rational factors and more human factors that impact the decision maker. In B2C marketing these human factors are included in what is referred to as Psychographics- attitudes,

✓	Inevitable
✓	Indelible
✓	Inviolate
	Indomitable
	Ingenious

Read Time: 2 min.

Priority: 2

Complexity to Enact: Low

beliefs, feelings, etc. Yes, it's the human stuff. It is in your Personas?

You Get It Often, half the battle is simply a matter of conveying that you understand what gets under the prospect's skin. It makes the prospect say: "They get me!", and we tend to trust the people that "get us". It relieves us from having to scrupulously question every claim. "They get me" is what lets you trust someone to pick the movie you're going to see, to set you up on a date, or to complete a task in a manner that will satisfy you.

I Trust You We all understand that there are no guarantees of course, especially about that date. But having a grasp of the attitudes, beliefs and feelings of the prospect means that as you present the well-reasoned justifications for purchase of your product, you can also convey that you understand their world, and thus can be trusted.

MORE Trust makes the sale 10x easier. Of course, the strongest trust comes from positive prior experiences with your company. But absent that (as with a new prospect), the best way to engender trust is by demonstrating that you "get" the prospect at the human level.

NEXT
What action can you take to try this for your business?
Jot a couple notes here:

_____

_____

_____

11 Focus on differentiation more than on polish in the creative work

WHY

"Professional-looking" is the way B2B marketers describe mar-com materials that suck. They have nice pictures and fonts and are competently laid-out, but they look pretty much like everyone else's mar-com stuff and communicate the same things. This will kill your smart, clear-eyed and differentiated messaging on the vine.

WHAT

- Constantly re-center your creatives on your core messages
- Reject cliché or distractingly 'cool' approaches
- Find inventive but rational creatives and let them run

HOW

Kill Cliché Kill the cliché and the generic. That includes the words you use, the stock pictures you select, the scenes you shoot, the claims you make, and the overall design you employ in promotional materials. If it looks and sounds like a lot of other things, prospects will assume that your product is pretty much the same as the other options.

Not Just Cool That said, the creative work must be an expression of your key differentiation- not just some designer's notion of "cool". Getting differentiated creative starts by assuring that you've attended to some of the other Rules, i.e.: understanding how you are differentiated from competition, knowing your value proposition and competitive position, assuring that the key messages are well-defined and clear, etc. This is the information you use to brief your creative types. You must make it crystal clear just what message they are to convey. Creative design is problem-solving. So, you've got to be very precise about the problem to be solved.

Common Issue: "This is very creative, and I love it, but I'm not sure it's fully on message."

Solution: Re-brief on the message and try anew.

✓ Inevitable

✓ Indelible

Inviolate

✓ Indomitable

Ingenious

 Read Time: 3 min.

 Priority: 2

(i) Complexity to Enact: Medium

Stay Back Once the creatives "get it", stay out of their way. There is no better way to nose-dive creative work than for a meddling client to "participate" in its development. If the team you are using is not creative enough to out-creative you by coming up with something that you would not have thought of, you need to find a new team. Sure, you can critique how well the work is conveying your differentiation and message, and you must. But don't give in to the temptation to play designer.

$ # ! Creative doesn't have to be expensive even though "professional-looking" creative can often be very expensive. If you must use in-house mar-com resources (as many B2B products do), you've got to find the gems in that department to work with. These are folks who are not routinized in the factory-style approach of too many mar-com departments and thus simply make everything look the same. Those "gems" are itching for a fresh challenge. Give it to them.

MORE Bottom line, your assessment criteria for creative must be:

- How clearly and impactfully does it communicate my message(s) to the prospect?
- How different does it look from the competition's creative, and does that look reinforce my differentiation?

"But my product is intentionally a 'me-too' offering at a cheaper price, not a differentiation play!"

Well then, likely it's your price that's different. So, portray that in a differentiated way... Value!

NEXT

What action can you take to try this for your business?

_____

_____

12 Be Brief

WHY Nuf said

HOW Edit, edit, edit.

MORE During the height of WWII, Winston Churchill wrote a long letter to a friend. The letter went on for pages and pages. Upon reading it the friend was struck by the fact that this most pivotal man had written this long letter at this most pivotal time history.

But the letter closed with an apology: "I'm sorry that this letter is so long. I didn't have time to make it shorter."

Being concise is far more difficult than being verbose. But prospects have little patience. Be brief.

NEXT

What action can you take to try this for your business?

Jot a very brief note here:

	Inevitable
	Indelible
✓	Inviolate
✓	Indomitable
	Ingenious

🕐 Not Done Yet?

📈 Priority: 1

ⓘ Complexity to Enact: Low

Leverage

Do what matters most

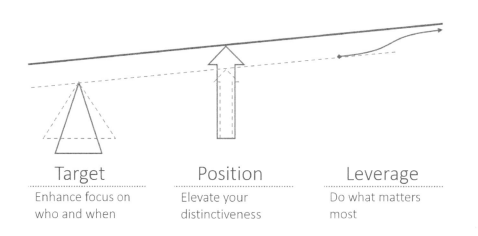

Target	Position	Leverage
Enhance focus on who and when	Elevate your distinctiveness	Do what matters most

13 Utilize account-based marketing to cultivate your most profitable customers

WHY
The Pareto principle (80/20 rule) works in just about everything, and this is no exception. In fact, it's likely that nearly 90% of your profits come from just 10% of your customers. And, of course, profits would be the point.

If you measure profitability, not just revenue, when you weight where your marketing spend is going to go, you'll find that a good part of your spending should go toward further cultivating either your most profitable customers, or companies that are quite similar to them.
That's what ABM is all about.

BTW- This is the warm-center of B2B marketing for the foreseeable future. Lead-gen is good, but this is money.

Inevitable

✓ Indelible

Inviolate

✓ Indomitable

✓ Ingenious

Read Time: 3 min.

Priority: 1

Complexity to Enact: High

WHAT
- Use a cross-disciplinary team to identify best customers who have green-space available
- Select one customer and treat it like a segment of its own to build sales-linked approaches that cultivate new business
- Assign resources and spend time working out the bugs
- Expand to additional customers over time

HOW
If you have a set of these 'best' customers that are big enough that they offer lots of uncultivated green space, that's your list. Pick 1 of them to get started, then expand the program as your approach matures.

If your 'best' customers don't have a lot of green space, you want to look for other companies that are similar to your 'best'. That's wickedly obvious, huh? But that means that you'll need to have a clear set of criteria about what constitutes a 'best' prospect. Pick meaningful criteria (e.g.: order volume/sales, company growth, structure, geography, use of competing products, etc.) and rate each prospect on each of the criteria you have chosen. Leverage actual data about the prospects to bring rigor to your ranking.

Look, there are entire books written about Account-based marketing. Read one. Meantime, do this:

1 Get a committee together, (sales/marketing/product represented) to discuss who your best customers are on the basis of overall profitability and who else is most like them.

2 Once you hash it out, focus on building account-specific tactics for one profitable customer that has greenfield-treating that customer as a market segment unto themselves. Build a marketing/sales plan that targets this extremely narrow niche with laser precision. And do it in partnership with sales. This must be a well-coordinated, team effort. ABM does not work without the direct involvement of sales.

MORE Having trouble getting consensus on who the best customers are? Use the Delphi method to rate prospects on key characteristics in order to leverage everyone's insights most effectively. Here's how:

First Establish a set of evaluative criteria (such as previously mentioned). Then ask everyone in your ABM committee to secretly rate each candidate customer on each criterion-scale 1-10, writing it down. Next, go around the table and have each person reveal their rating for a criterion, explaining why they rated in the way they did. Let the group absorb the logic and assumptions of others and discuss as desired.

Then Once the logic of each person has been heard and considered by everyone in the group, ask them to re-rate the criteria. Rinse and repeat. What happens is that the group quickly starts coming together—because each member comes to see issues and logic from others that they may not have considered or weighted appropriately on their own. After a couple rounds, you'll have a pretty good consensus.

NEXT

What action can you take to try this for your business?

_____

14 Focus on quality in your content marketing

WHY
Everyone is already awash in content—far, far too much to read or use. So, the content that you develop must be extremely concise, very specific as to purpose and to how the reader can use it.

WHAT
- Focus your content on immediate customer problems, carefully targeted
- Cut back your frequency to make your content more special
- Try new mediums
- Then, when ready to purchase, pour on the information

HOW
The question to answer is **NOT**: "What information do we have that might be of interest to our customers?"

The question **IS**: "What difficulties are our customers/prospects suffering with right now about which we can provide useable information?"

That's a very different question, because prospects may be "interested" in many things, but they will only take time to review information regarding issues of immediate need and significance.

Abundance Cheapens
Look, we are all experts at ignoring information that is not relevant to the stuff that is truly important to us. We swipe past, or simply ignore, hundreds of messages every day. There is no shortage of email in the in-box. So, whatever "content" you want to use for marketing purposes, it must offer enough real relevance and utility to get past the hardened filters in your prospect's mind.

Moreover, if you are the company that deluges prospects with endless newsletters and announcements, your messages will begin to be deleted without so much as reading the

✓	Inevitable
	Indelible
✓	Inviolate
	Indomitable
	Ingenious

 Read Time: 4 min.

 Priority: 2

 Complexity to Enact: Low

headline. You've just turned your content marketing effort into a **customer alienation program**.

So, don't talk at prospects just to be talking. If you speak-up, have something to say that is truly useful, then pause. Make them look forward to the next golden nugget you bestow upon them, rather than dread "yet another newsletter from those guys."

This also means that the person you have writing all that newsletter content- who was never in the prospect's business nor actually sold a product to such a prospect- would best be doing something else instead. Even if you give them a nice set of 'key words' or 'messages' to focus on, it's bound to end up sounding like 'marketing-speak' and won't really deliver information that is of significant value to the prospect.

Try a New Medium

A different kind of experience for your content can help. Create something other than a written document—a video, learning module, working spreadsheet, a little app, etc. As long as you are not feverishly struggling to get out a newsletter every week (or every day), put some effort into making what you do put out, (at a less feverish rate), in order to increase its impact and value.

This is not to say that there isn't a place for white papers and study data. With such substantive vehicles, the weight of the material tends to give it credence as being "valuable".

But the novelty of a different medium can also cut-through.

Let Them Bathe

While you don't want to pester prospects with 'content', at the final decision-making phase in the buying process prospects tend to want to 'bathe' in the details. Think of the last time you bought a car. First you noticed cars in ads or on the road, then you looked at some cars on dealer lots, later test drove a few different cars... and then what? You

Content
Without
Relevant
Impact is
Just Noise

collected brochures (or websites) from the finalists and examined the information and pictures of every little feature with great relish. You bathed in the information. You enjoyed the process, because you were ready to be convinced. And when you rose from your bath, your decision was made.

So, it is important to assure that when your prospect is ready to bathe you have all the water and bubble bath they crave, ready and accessible. Note that if you push this out to them too early they will ignore it, or even be annoyed by it. But when they are ready, they want it all at once.

Make sure this information is collected and easily accessible. This is a place where your website can really shine.

MORE   What constitutes quality content? It's the same old stuff: Relevance, Differentiation, Credibility. But also, usability, design, and especially brevity in our content-overloaded world.

Relevant
Differentiated
Credible

NEXT

What action can you take to try this for your business?

Jot a couple notes here:

_____

_____

_____

_____

"Either write
something
worth reading
or do
something
worth writing."

Benjamin
Franklin

15 Don't badger B2B prospects

WHY

As previously stated, we are all awash in "communications". Getting yet another unsolicited, incessant message from a vendor is not likely to win you points. In fact, it can even turn-off the prospect to any future messages you may send. Then where will you be?

It's a delicate balance. Too few, and you risk being forgotten. Too many, and you look desperate. Never a good look. But how much is too much?

WHAT

- Establish a planned and measured cadence in your communications with prospects

HOW

Take a measured approach that is less likely to overwhelm by sending only information that is relevant to the customer acquisition stage your prospect is in.
(See Rule: Map the customer's journey to understand when and how you can exert influence.)

Plan Your Work

For each stage, make only a pre-determined number of contacts at intervals that are based upon the prospect's response (or lack thereof). Each successive message should be less insistent than the last and should not repeat information previously delivered. (However, you can refer to such information.)

The essence of each message is a suggestion of the best, next action they can take, or an offer to provide additional information that may be of help to prospects in their stage. Don't send a continuous barrage of testimonials, feature or benefit descriptions, or comparison charts. It gets tedious.

Neither should you send a steady stream of new offers, because with each successive offer prospects either lose interest, or if they are still interested they may intentionally

Inevitable

✓ Indelible

✓ Inviolate

Indomitable

Ingenious

Read Time: 2 min.

Priority: 2

Complexity to Enact: Low

wait to hear the next (potentially better) offer to come. Thus, they never take action on your offer, but might take action on a well-timed offer from your competitor.

Don't Overwork Your Plan

Remember that your goal is to move the prospect to the next stage. After your predetermined number of contacts for a given stage, you've got to be willing to stop beating that horse and simply recycle him into a future follow-up file. In other words, if you can't move the prospect to the next stage with your set program, don't burn them down with annoying over-persistence that will kill any future opportunity you may have with them. Realize that one of two conditions exist: Either the prospect is simply not ready to move and would be best approached at a later date, or your tactics need to be improved. Disheartening as this may be, take the hint and rework the approach.

"But this approach worked with a lot of other prospects" you say. Then the question is: what is different about the prospects with whom it did not work? What factor have you missed? Go back to your segments and personas and determine if there is some element that is different among these prospects which requires a different approach.

MORE The old adage is: Doing the same thing over and over while expecting a new result is the very definition of insanity.

NEXT
What action can you take to try this for your business?
Jot a couple notes here:

_____

_____

> "People say we live in an age of information overload. Right? I don't know about that, but I just know that I get too many marketing emails."
> James Veitch

16 Mind the prospect's experience when you ask them to respond to your messages

WHY You only get one chance to make a good first impression.

Your promotional material (email, ad, brochure, etc.) includes a call-to-action, right? e.g., visit website, register, attend the webinar, call, etc. You are spending a lot of effort and money to get prospects to take that action. But if your prospect's user experience in taking that action is clunky, confusing, or otherwise problematic, you just wasted your effort.

Prospects are impatient and hyper-critical, and this is their first opportunity to know you. Creating a poor impression with them makes them lose their interest at best, and at worst, makes them dismiss your company as "difficult" to work with. You won't get that prospect back anytime soon.

WHAT
- Carefully map the path and the steps customers must follow to respond to your messages, and simplify
- Use competitor processes as benchmarks, and improve upon them

HOW **Keep it Real**

Real Simple Start by making sure that what you are asking them to do is dirt simple and easy. No one wants to jump through hoops on behalf of a vendor. For example, provide a very, very simple form they use to request information- 'simple' meaning: just ask for their email, not their biography. Following the initial response stage, you can start to get more personal, but not on a first date.

Moreover, make sure that the action you are asking for does not lead to something they'll perceive as intrusive. Too often, companies want to engage with the prospect directly upon first introduction, but prospects may be put-off by this. The prospect may not be ready for full engagement and wants to keep their distance. Keeping the response experience simple

✓ Inevitable

Indelible

✓ Inviolate

Indomitable

Ingenious

Read Time: 5 min.

Priority: 1

Complexity to Enact: Medium

and low-pressure creates comfort and openness to later entreaties.

Keep the language simple too. Use the language of your prospect, not industry jargon or vacuous superlatives. As in all marketing, you are speaking to a human being. Your Personas should help you to gauge the right kind of language to use. (See Rule: Refine personas around key B2B attributes, so your messages resonate)

Real Responsive However simple the action is to take, if you don't provide immediate affirmation of their action, they assess that you are not responsive. Even if your follow-up is understood to take a little time, you must at least acknowledge their request immediately. How fast does a response have to be? Well, if you are online, how long does it take you to navigate to a competitor to see what they have to offer? Automated responses are called for in this instance, e.g., an email or text.

If it is going to take more than a few minutes to respond, count-down messages are in order. Let the prospect know just how long your response is going to take. Follow-up messages that count-down the time remaining can help, particularly if the delay is a couple days. Just don't overdo it. Further, don't promise to respond in "under" a certain amount of time, e.g.: "You'll receive your custom link in less than 10 minutes". Your prospect will assume that this means it will appear in the smallest imaginable amount of time that's under your maximum delay. You're saying: 'Less than 10', but they are thinking: 'OK, a couple minutes'. Then, after three minutes they are already disappointed. Instead say: "You'll receive your custom link 10 minutes from now". Then, when you actually deliver it in 4 minutes, they will be delighted. "Under-promise and over-deliver" is a cliché for good reason.

Real Valuable Seriously consider adding something of immediate value to what you are asking them to do. Believe it or not, getting additional promotional literature or a call from your sales team may not be all that appealing to a prospect,

Keep it
* Simple
* Responsive
* Valuable

despite their apparent interest in your product. Provide some kind of instant gratification to go with it, e.g.: a downloadable report with some useful information, (but information that isn't just promo material masquerading as a 'report'.)
(See Rule: Focus on quality in your content marketing)

Bottom line, you want the prospect to say: "Well, that was easy and pretty useful!" Implicit in that thought is the feeling that your company is easy to do business with, values their time, and provides immediate value. That's a nice first date.

Map Out the Response Flow in Detail

You need to be explicit about the specific steps that prospects take when they are responding to you. The Customer Journey Map was discussed previously, and you can think of this effort as drilling into the details for one part of the overall map.
(See Rule: Map the customer's journey to understand when and how you can exert influence.)

Get Granular

Be Granular Mapping the response flow involves charting each step, action, and response- flow-chart style. You show the branches in the flow and each action down each branch in their planned sequences. Establishing the **timing** for each action is important to understanding the temporal flow of the prospect's experience. You also need to note the **mechanisms** that support or actuate each step, because these are often the 'long-poles.' (Those mechanisms may introduce response delay or might delay the whole thing due to how long it takes you to build the systems initially.)

The map must offer a very granular view of things. You need to account for every step, however small, that the prospect will experience. Take nothing for granted. It is always within the sphere of assumed understanding that critical problems in planning arise. You can't assume your team's understanding. You've got to document it, so everyone sees the same thing, and so everyone has an opportunity to judge what may go wrong.

Involve a Team While you should start with a draft, this is another exercise best done with friends. Draw it on a whiteboard to map the granular actions that prospects take in response to your call-to-action, flagging the timing and the mechanisms relied upon along the way. This whiteboard session can be short (for a very simple response), or a few hours for a more complex one. As with other team sessions, the point is both to gain the insights that come from multiple perspectives and minds, and to build common understanding and buy-in to the approach you are mapping out.

The result can take any form you like, though simpler is always better. You may find that this work helps to inform the larger Customer Journey Map and may lead to improvements to that work too. Great.

Benchmark

Competitive Benchmarks The quest for understanding just how simple, responsive, and valuable your process must be should be taken from the benchmark your competitors are setting. Yes, that means you are going to have to go through their processes, or get someone to do so, noting the experience in detail. These are the benchmarks that your prospects will measure you against, so you must measure yourself against them in advance. When doing this there are usually distinct differences in approach which lead to self-justifications like: *"But our approach is also doing X so of course it isn't as timely."*; or: *"We can't do that because we have to use our 'Y' system."* This gets you nowhere. Reframe this discussion around your larger goals that have to do with the overall experience. Enumerate and weight the pros and cons of the overall competitor process and compare it to your own. Be sure you understand which moments are the most pivotal within the flow, (those where you risk losing the prospect, or at least risk turning them off).

MORE This is critical. Spend the effort to get it right.

NEXT

What action can you take to try this for your business?

17 Measure what's important (Not everything is actually important)

WHY

Your marketing automation system or other tracking mechanisms give you a lot of data. But data is not knowledge and it doesn't help you decide what to do unless you can properly wrap your arms around it.

In short, you must identify and focus on just those few things that truly impact the business.

WHAT

- When selecting your KPIs, edit the list by answering these questions for each option you consider:
  - What does this likely tell us about the direction and health of our marketing efforts?
  - What can we do as a result of seeing this measure?

HOW

Obviously, there is no shortage of things to track, and all have some value. But while you may be able to track rather a lot of things successfully, you must be able to boil that down to a few key metrics that really signal how on-target and healthy your marketing efforts are. This will vary for different businesses, so we will not attempt to make a pronouncement about the "ideal" metrics to track. That's a fool's errand. It is you who must decide what specific metrics are appropriate for your particular business. In fact, those metrics will likely differ even from your direct competitors.

✓ Inevitable
✓ Indelible
Inviolate
Indomitable
✓ Ingenious

Read Time: 4 min.

Priority: 2

Complexity to Enact: Medium

Some of the many things that are "important":

- Impressions
- Brand awareness
- PR mentions
- Outbound campaign volume
- Open rates
- Click rates
- Web site visits
- Webinar attendance
- Followers, likes, re-tweets, etc.
- Conference badge swipes, appointments, demos

- Qualified leads (from each source)
- Cost per lead
- Requests for information
- Pipeline leads
- Sales calls completed
- Demonstrations delivered
- RFPs received
- Proposals delivered
- Sales completed
- Sales closing rate
- Total cost per sale
- Average contract price
- Average contract margin
- Lifetime customer value
- Market penetration

And on and on...

Use Only a Limited Number of KPIs that are Truly Meaningful

Selecting KPIs

You want to end up with **3-5 metrics** to use as your core KPIs. Having more than this makes them difficult to interpret, as well as being too numerous to incorporate within the larger, business-wide KPI measures.

Criteria To decide on the metrics you should measure, assess your candidates against these three criteria:

1 Measures are linked to core business goals
   - The goal financials tell part of the story, but the other part has to do with strategy, e.g., Is our strategy to grow within existing markets or new ones? With existing or new products? Average deal size or volume? Skimming profits or seeking a large footprint? Etc.
   - The metrics must give an indication of success toward the business strategy and goals.

2 Measures are understandable and clear to all
   - Must not be complicated or ambiguous, and must be able to be expressed simply, (fits on one slide.)

- Your team, peers, executives and the board must be able to understand the metric. Really understand it.

3   Measured changes must imply causes and be actionable
- Noting the change in a metric has no value unless one can infer why it has changed, and then take action as a result (to continue or halt the trend).

Indicates What? To reiterate, when you look at these core KPIs, you should be able to answer these questions:
- What does this likely tell us about the direction and health of our marketing efforts?
- What can we do as a result of seeing this measure?

MORE   You won't know whether a metric is truly giving you the insight you need until you live with it for a while. As such, don't be hesitant to change your KPI metrics if something isn't working out. There can be a lot of inertia that holds back such a change, e.g.: *"Well, how will we track over time if we keep changing the metrics?"* However, loyally tracking the same, useless metrics over a long period of time simply says that you are not paying attention. So, pay attention, and change quickly if needed.

Change Metrics as You Learn More About What is Truly Meaningful

NEXT

What action can you take to try this for your business?

Jot a couple notes here:

_____

_____

_____

_____

"Just because
you *can*
measure
everything
doesn't mean
that
you *should*."

W. Edward
Deming

18 Optimize sales enablement by using a partnership-driven feedback loop

WHY
Sales is Marketing's #1 customer.

"No, no, no... Sales is not our customer! They constantly insist that all the deals we lose are due to features, price, or because our literature sucks. It's like they never heard the phrase: 'The selling starts when you hear No.' And they don't even use the material we give them anyway!"

You see how this goes nowhere?

If Sales is not successful, Marketing is not successful in B2B. Period. It's like a marriage. There is misinterpretation of action, lack of communication, plenty of opportunity for frustration. But if you can make it work- Bliss. If you can't- Hell. What's more, there is no divorcing Sales. You have to make it work.

WHAT
- Create a sales-centered journey map to identify the key opportunities for sales enablement elements
- Establish a rotating sales roundtable to elicit continuous, participatory discussion with sales (instead of just demands)

HOW
You've got to create a partnership-driven feedback loop with sales. Otherwise, there is just a long list of stuff that sales want, might need, and probably won't use. Meanwhile, both parties continue talking past each other.

You know the tools that are often on that list, all of which are at least potentially valuable. But you can't do them all:

Read Time: 5 min.

Priority: 1

Complexity to Enact: Medium

- Customizable product presentation decks
- Product brochures
  - Product literature per product and product line
  - Product Specification cut sheets
  - Contract terms overview

So Many Options, So Little Time

- (Brief and long versions in both print and digital)
- Company overview brochures
  - About the company, product line breadth, support and related issues
- White Papers
  - Detailing customer applications and viability/success of your solutions
- Specialized web pages/sites
  - For particular sales teams/ regions, customer categories, or specialized direct response
  - Providing self-service tools and resources for customers
- Battle Cards
  - Providing details about how to sell against specific competitors
  - How to handle specific objections or needs
- Play Books
  - Detailing how to identify and pursue specific kinds of customers
- Sales team briefing sessions
  - Live or web-based overview presentation of product features/benefits, roll-out, support, marketing programs, etc. to inform sales
  - Periodic update reports
- Product training
  - Live or web-based training on how to present the product, for various audiences
- Customer feedback reports
- And more…

Sound familiar? No, you can't do it all, nor can sales use it all. Note too, this list does not even include the marketing programs that generate awareness and leads for sales.

So, what's a marketer to do?

Create a Sales-Centered Journey Map

You have to establish that partnership-driven feedback loop on the back of a tangible artifact- a sales-centered customer journey map.

To create that initial map, work with sales leadership and a couple of the best sales staff to hash it out together. Use the journey map model previously discussed to focus on how sales interact with prospects & customers within each segment and for each Persona that requires a different process. (See Rule: Map the customer's journey to understand when and how you can exert influence.)

This intensive discussion(s) will reveal what really happens throughout the sales process, which resources really get used or not used, and where gaps exist. You establish a common language with sales, understand the key articulation points in the sales process, and thus can then talk specifically about what can better support the sales team.

In the end, the priorities will become clear to everyone. Moreover, you've also established a baseline from which ongoing discussions can stem—the journey map anchors discussion, rather than simply orbiting this week's wish list.

Focus on the Specific Events of the Customer's Journey

Establish a Rotating Sales Roundtable

Set up a regular sales roundtable session (at least quarterly) to hash through what is working or not working and how the customer world or competitive tactics may have changed that suggests the need for something new.

You should have a core group for these sessions (representing marketing, sales, CS, and perhaps others), but should invite one or two extra sales people to participate in each session in order to keep things fresh. These folks participate for one session, then are replaced in the next.

The session focuses on the sales-centric journey map. This keeps the discussion focused and results in a changed map where everyone can see and agree to the key influence points and tactics needed for each event in the customer's journey.

To gain enthusiasm from sales for these sessions, keep the focus positive. Ask for sales success stories. Everyone loves to share their successes. It makes them feel expert and highlights their accomplishments. You use discussion of those stories to dissect the elements that created success, and which may create success in other situations as well. Everyone wins.

With this kind of regular, refreshed, and focused dialog, the discussion changes from *"We need a full brochure with everything in it!"*, to something more like:

Fuel Sales Partnership with Success Stories

"So, at this point in the process the prospect is typically assessing us against competitors as part of their evaluation committee. So, what have you seen that works best? How can we make sure every committee actually gets just most critical comparative information/ demo/ thought leadership/ etc. that will make our advantage apparent?"

That's the kind of focused dialog you want with sales. The kind that is partnership-driven.

MORE   Hang out with sales people. Get to know them and establish mutual trust. You will learn far more about the intricacies of prospects and the nature of the challenges faced than your CRM system can ever give you.

(But, yes, you've got to look at the CRM data too.)

NEXT

What action can you take to try this for your business?

19 Qualify leads the way you prioritize segments

WHY
After sorting leads by their market segment, there must be a consistent way of establishing the quality of leads for follow-up. The Segment Prioritization criteria you have already established can serve this purpose well and helps keep priorities aligned from the start to the finish of the customer's journey.

WHAT
- Specify your focus of follow-up efforts based upon the prospect's match to your segment prioritization criteria

HOW
Recall the Segment Prioritization Criteria previously discussed and the modifications you've made to it in order to suit your product and market. (You have done that, right?)
(See Rule: Segment more carefully than you already have.)

These criteria were valuable in assigning priority to the segments that you are addressing. They are likewise valuable for the process of assigning value to leads, (lead qualification.)

Here is the list of segmentation prioritization options we've recommended that are also relevant to the task of qualifying leads, (though yours may vary.) Leverage these criteria to establish the appropriate follow-up for the lead that is consistent with your segment priorities.

- Psychographic
  - Awareness (High, Medium, Low)
  - Ability to Purchase (High, Medium, Low)
- Competitive
  - Differentiation Strength (High, Medium, Low)
  - Competitors (A, B, C)
- Behavioral
  - Unmet Needs (High, Medium, Low)
  - Purchase Urgency (High, Medium, Low)

To gather this kind of insight you can put these criteria on your lead forms (trade show, telemarketing, sales reports,

---

✓ Inevitable

Indelible

✓ Inviolate

Indomitable

Ingenious

🕐 Read Time: 3 min.

📈 Priority: 2

ⓘ Complexity to Enact: Low

etc.) to gain the direct assessment of those who are gathering leads in the first place. For leads that come without such insight, they can be later characterized within your pipeline list by adding the criteria to the lead profile data you track.

Either way, when leads come in, rate each on these criteria (whatever is known at the time.) Later, as follow-up on the lead proceeds this information can be flushed-out and updated to reflect the prospect's current status regarding each criterion.

Follow-up Approach The criteria serve to qualify the lead in useful ways that help you decide what to communicate and what to do with the lead. Of course, you can adapt these criteria as suitable to your product/ market. But the following offer a good starting point:

Create consistency between segment and lead prioritization

Criteria	Rating	Follow-up Focus
Awareness	High	Focus on differentiation
	Medium	Focus on target benefits
	Low	Focus on explaining core product capabilities & benefits
Ability to Purchase	High	Prioritize follow-up
	Medium	Assess if this may improve in future
	Low	Assess real customer potential
Competitor(s)	A	(Assign a priority to each competitor based upon strategy)
	B	
	C	
Differentiation Strength	High	Emphasize differentiators
	Medium	Expand on the differentiation story
	Low	Emphasize value, or product ecosystem factors
Unmet Needs	High	Prioritize follow-up
	Medium	Medium priority
	Low	Deprioritize
Purchase Urgency	High	Top priority
	Medium	Frequent & regular follow-up
	Low	Consider special offers

Obviously, there are other relevant factors to consider in lead qualification. Similarly, sometimes the follow-up focus related to separate criteria may end up being in conflict with each other, e.g.: 'Awareness' is 'High' signaling the need to 'focus on differentiation', but 'Differentiation Strength' is 'Low' signaling a need to 'emphasize value or product ecosystem factors'. In such cases you need to decide which criteria takes precedence. In this case, it is likely that 'Differentiation Strength' will have a greater impact on the sales potential of the lead, so I'd go with the later follow-up recommendation. But these are judgement calls that will improve with experience.

The overall idea is to align your lead qualification with your segment prioritization to the greatest extent possible so as to achieve greater consistency in how you evaluate opportunities. And, because these criteria are transparent, you can have a substantive discussion about them with sales.

Tune Your Criteria Over Time

MORE

The process of tuning the criteria to your product and market is, as always, up to you.

No doubt you have existing qualification criteria, including those included within any CRM system that you may employ. It is not necessary to redo everything in order to add the clarity that this type of criteria offer. It can be an additive process. Moreover, you want to continuously fine tune your criteria based upon what you learn about the factors that are most valuable in your market space. (Sound familiar?)

NEXT

What action can you take to try this for your business?

Jot a couple notes here:

_____

_____

Awareness

Ability to
Purchase

Differentiation

Competitors

Unmet Needs

Purchase
Urgency

20 Be a Marketing Mensch

WHY

What's a "mensch"?

Derived from the Yiddish word "mentsh", it's a person of integrity and honor.

Effective B2B marketing does not rely on gimmicks, loose claims, or spectacular offers sent by faux Nigerian princes. The quickest ways to be discredited by prospects is to spam them, make hyperbolic claims, or somehow trick them into responding to an offer.

You never, never, never get those prospects back.

So be a mensch.

HOW

Well. Just be honest and fair in your marketing. (Don't spam the email, claim relationships you don't have, etc.)

Provide proof for your claims, e.g., study data, surveys, testimonials, etc. All this makes your message believable, and in turn, makes it easier to believe in your product.

MORE

You get it. Don't you?

NEXT

What action can you take to try this for your business?

Jot a couple notes here:

_____

_____

_____

✔	Inevitable
✔	Indelible
✔	Inviolate
✔	Indomitable
	Ingenious

Read Time: 1 min.

Priority: 1

Complexity to Enact: Low

_____

_____

_____

"Being honest
may not get
you a lot of
friends, but it'll
always get you
the right
ones."

John Lennon

_____

_____

_____

_____

_____

21 PR does not stand for "Press Release"

WHY   Public Relations can be a powerful tool in B2B, but to make it work you've got to manage a well-rounded effort.

No— just posting press releases to press release brokers doesn't cut it. Just how many press releases do you think come across the publisher's desk of your industry's key journal each day? See how silly it is to simply loft releases into the ether and call it PR?

To be effective, you've got to make PR a program, not an afterthought.

WHAT
- Stop letting PR efforts be press-release-driven
- Establish meaningful stories you want to pitch, then work a set of target outlets to whom you'll pitch them
- Leverage trade shows for their many PR opportunities
- Hire a resource to handle the intricacies of your program

HOW   In a B2B space, Public Relations is better thought of as "Audience Relations" because you are usually not interested in reaching the general public. Your interest lies with the narrowly focused target audience for your solutions and with the goal of changing the audience's awareness of, or attitudes about, an issue that is closely related to your solutions.

The operative question is then: How do we reach our audience with 'earned media,' (that is: media coverage that you don't pay for directly?) Even more to the point, how can we leverage such earned media to influence our target audience in a way that spurs interest and pulls prospects toward us without using direct advertising/promotion? Now That's PR!

✓ Inevitable
✓ Indelible
✓ Inviolate
Indomitable
Ingenious

Read Time: 8 min.

Priority: 2

Complexity to Enact: High

What's the Story

Effective PR (think: 'Audience Relations') is all about building an interesting story around your product space, then propagating that story through as many 3rd party vehicles as possible. Interesting stories are not usually about products. They are about the key issues or problems that surround the people for which your product is a solution. So, while the latest product release or customer acquired may urge the generation of a release (e.g., Your CEO says: "Let's get a release out on that!"), this kind of subject matter usually does not constitute a very interesting story to the members of your audience. To them, it just sounds like more: "blah, blah, blah from a vendor."

Step Back Take a step back from the particulars to see the bigger picture. What key issue are we addressing that is meaningful to the audience? Why does it need to be addressed? Who thinks so? Is this issue new or long-standing? What is the scope of its impact? Etc. In the answers to these questions is the essence of the PR story you can tell.

PR stories are about key issues that surround the people for whom your product is a solution

Example

An effective story could be shaped using the following basic structure (though this is not the only approach):

- Important issue that you should be aware of. (Topic fits within the editorial interests of your target publications.)
- Key impacts of the issue and why it is important to address this issue now.
- Authoritative voices chime in to reinforce. They describe the kind of solution that can be effective. This just happens to be your kind of solution.

PR Program Factors

There are many correct ways to construct a PR program. Here is a core framework to use. Obviously, you will adapt and enhance this base approach to accommodate the particulars of your product/market space. There's plenty of room for creative variance and expansion in the approach.

Objectives First, establish objectives for the PR program.
You are likely seeking to influence the same people you have
targeted with your broader marketing plan. So, the question
is: who can be reached/influenced via earned media more
effectively than via more direct promotional vehicles? This
should have shown-up in your journey-mapping and persona
work. (You did that, right?)
(See Rule: Map the customer's journey to understand when and
how you can exert influence)
(See Rule: Refine personas around key B2B attributes, so your
messages resonate)

In what way do you want to influence them? That is: why
would they care, why will the influence matter to you, and
what do you want them to do as a result? Be clear. e.g.: *"We
want their fear to be sparked by understanding the risks
posed by this issue, then request our thought-leader white
paper on the subject."*

A reminder: your PR objectives must blend seamlessly with
your broader marketing objectives.

Where to Reach Out Knowing who you want to reach,
and what effect you wish to have, determine what vehicles
are best able to touch your target. Make a list of these and
rank them in terms of reach and influence. These may include
trade publications, websites, blogs and other social media
outlets, analysts, etc. Again, determine the reach that each
has (how many people in your target are reached), and how
influential it is (i.e.: from trusted authority to passing
opinion). Note that today content is distributed first and
foremost online. So, think about the online presentation of
your story first.

Don't discount the value of peer viewpoints when assessing
outlets. Peer experiences and opinions hold great sway with
those trying to narrow a plethora of options down to a select
few. Still, while social media (Facebook, Linked-in, Twitter,
Instagram, etc.) are often viewed as "must have" PR vehicles,

PR Program
Factors
 • Objectives
 • Where
 • Stories
 • The Pitch

be deliberate in your consideration of their value for your target audience. For example: Are target prospects actually likely to 'follow' your product or company Facebook page, or even to be taken to it by cross-links? Is that where you want customers to go for information about you, or do you want them at your website? (Hint: 'your website' is the answer.)

Social media can be an important vehicle, but you've got to be clear about what you expect from it. Typically, you want to "listen in" to the social media dialog happening within your key channels to understand both what is of interest/ debate/ concern, and so you can interject something suitable into the exchange. There are tools for doing just this sort of thing. But beware, commercial-sounding posts will quickly earn the ire of those you had wished to influence.

Stories

* Case Studies
* Profiles
* Research Studies
* Trends
* Executive Presentations

Story Devices What devices can be used to effectively tell your story? There are many choices: Case histories, people profiles, research studies, thought leader trend analysis, executive presentations, etc. Some of these likely also offer supporting evidence for your core messaging.

The written word is usually the first option considered, but also consider if could you tell your story in a different medium that might be more accessible, compelling or appealing to your target.

The Pitch Why do publications want such stories? Quite simply, B2B publication editors generally don't have staff writers. They pay outside writers for their editorial content by commissioning articles. If you can provide the editor with an article that is written to read like the publication's other content, and if it is also interesting to their readers, the editor is interested.

Note those caveats: the story must be interesting, objective, and written in the publication's voice (not your company's voice). In order to understand these factors, you need to speak with the editor to get a feel for what he/she is looking for and to understand the publication's acceptance criteria for articles. They are only interested in topics that fit their target subject matter and perspective, and which can fit into a space on their editorial calendar. Still, the prospect of free content that can accommodate their standards is quite appealing.

That said, editors also understand that publications need money to run. So, proposing a package that includes an allocation of paid advertising can grease-the-skids of acceptance and buy some latitude.

Of course, the editor may want to write their own article to tell your story. Great. Just understand, this involves a lot of hand-holding.

The Trade Show

Trade shows are the mother-of-all-PR opportunities, expressly because there are so many ways to leverage the trade show event to create PR exposure.

The trade show is the mother-of-all-PR opportunities

Options abound:
- Construct a thought leader or executive presentation and get them on the speaker program, or in a satellite event.
- Publish a white paper, research study or opinion leader editorial. Propagate it in the show publication, as giveaways, bag stuffers, and in door drops.
- Hold an event for the trade publications and feed them wine and shrimp while they mill about with your executives and invited thought leaders.
- Set-up appointments with all the publications and have your briefing sheet ready to outline the stories you want to pitch.

The trade show is a perfect opportunity to artfully blend more direct "marketing" tactics with more indirect PR efforts. Moreover, the follow-up to the show is just as important. You must assure that those who became aware of the issues relevant to your product space can easily access the information they want. Likewise, you want to follow-up with publications and other outlets met during the show to emphasize the relevance of your topics to the post-show audience.

Hiring a Resource

Obviously, pulling-off all of this is quite a complex and time-consuming task. Which is why you should consider hiring a resource (full time or an outside expert) to handle it all.

If hiring an outside resource, size matters. Generally, B2B firms are best served by smaller PR vendors because the process and overhead of large firms make them uneconomical for the focused efforts of B2B firms.

Can the PR resource deliver value even within your focused target audience?

How much does industry experience count? Experience will give your resource a jump-start by knowing the industry terminology, publications, and key issues, all of which is quite valuable. However, this knowledge can be developed by a talented resource who has demonstrated expertise at putting effective programs together- though it may take longer to do so initially.

When interviewing a resource, be sure to ask them how they will approach building a PR program and listen for the answer. Don't tell them what you want- they'll just repeat that back to you.

MORE

Sound overwhelming? Yep. That last bit about hiring a resource may be your ticket—if you've got the budget. If not, pick one thing that you can pull off with existing resources. No, that does not mean writing a press release on the latest feature and sending it out to the wires... Did you actually read any part of this Rule?

NEXT
What action can you take to try this for your business?

_____

_____

What's Your Rule? _____

WHY _____
_____

WHAT · _____
· _____
· _____

HOW _____

_____

_____

_____

MORE _____

_____

_____

☐ Inevitable

☐ Indelible

☐ Inviolate

☐ Indomitable

☐ Ingenious

🕐 Read Time: _____

📈 Priority: _____

ⓘ Complexity to
Enact: _____

Don't be stingy...

Share your Rule at:
21b2bRules.com

NEXT
What action can you take to try this for your business?
Jot a couple notes here:

_____

_____

_____

Don't be stingy

Share your
RULE at:
21b2bRules.com

_____

_____

_____

_____

Glossary

Inevitable Unavoidable

Indelible Lasting

Inviolate Pure

Indomitable Impossible to defeat

Ingenious Cleverly and originally devised and well suited to its purpose (Rather like this book itself)

TAM Total Available Market = The total market demand for the product

SAM Serviceable Available Market = The portion of the TAM that you can or are targeting that is within your geographical reach

SOM Serviceable Obtainable Market = The portion of SAM that you expect to be able to actually capture

Growth Annualized Growth Rate

ACP Average Contract Price (or Average Contract Revenue if you prefer) = How much money you bring in on an average sale to the segment

ACM Average Contract Margin = How much gross profit margin is in that ACP

Champion One who is an active and vocal advocate for your product

Influential One who's opinions are considered to be authoritative and thus is looked to for guidance

Communicator One who spreads information liberally, though not necessarily with authority

Whinging To complain persistently and in a peevish or irritating way

* Don't understand some other term used in this book? Fortunately, there is this wonderful thing where you can get basic information about most anything. It's called: "The Internet" [visit: www.(anything you can think-up).com

Appendix

The Chasm Model: A model of product adoption created by Geoffrey Moore that describes key characteristics for several typical groups of potential customers based upon their willingness to adopt a new solution. These groups are generally defined as follows:

- **Innovators** (or Technologists): Are enthusiastic about any innovation and are willing to put up with very unrefined early product versions in order to try them
- **Early Adopters**: Want to be the first on their block, but won't bend over backwards to get it
- **Pragmatists** (or Early Majority): Need the product solution to be able to be practically applied to their work/life, but are willing to adjust their world in order to gain the solution's benefits
- **Conservatives** (or Late Majority): Insist that any new solution fit right into their present world, and that the solution is fully vetted and supported
- **Laggards**: Won't adopt a new solution without some heavy bludgeoning, or without discovering that their prior solution is no longer available

Read Moore's book: *Crossing the Chasm*, if you haven't already.

Needs/Pains/Gains: Borrows from the 'Jobs/Pains/Gains' model presented in Alex Osterwalder's book: *Value Proposition Design*. Another good read. In turn, the 'Jobs to be Done' concept has a few progenitors, notably Clay Christensen.

The Obligatory Author Bio

His 25+ years of executive experience includes VP Product/Marketing roles within 2- $1B+ companies, within smaller firms, and within a large-scale start-up. Bill also held executive positions at a software development firm and at an award-winning marketing communications agency.

In more than a decade of consulting work Bill has completed over 90 projects for clients ranging from medical information to manufacturing, helping business and product leaders to pinpoint market opportunities, plan customer solutions, and prepare both people and products for market success.

(That must be an old picture)

Thanks

"Hey, this wasn't in the table-of-contents!"

You are correct. Think of it as a bonus.

Thanks to those who helped me with the content, the editing, the design, and clear perspective:

John Viviano, John Schrefer, Rich Murphy, Steve Littlejohn, Laura Herlihy, Paul Heirendt, Kelly Haines, Brian Bussey and critical others (you know who you are)

Book Information

"Hey, this wasn't in the table-of-contents either!"

Again, you are correct. Just appreciate all the bonuses I'm giving you.

Want your own copy of this book? Don't be a cheapskate and just borrow your colleague's copy. How embarrassing. You can get your very own copy in the ordinary way. (You know- buy it.)

"Outside of a dog, a book is man's best friend. Inside of a dog it's too dark to read."
Groucho Marx

The Pitch

Do you need help with any of this stuff? We thought you'd never ask...

Bottom Line—you can't do B2B well if you don't have solid fundamentals in place first. ARCHIMEDESb2b lets you establish those fundamentals quickly with a focused combination of intensive workshops and follow-up.

Target
Enhance focus on
who and when

Position
Elevate your
distinctiveness

Leverage
Do what matters
most

ARCHIMEDESb2b.com

"I am outraged by this obvious promotional message right within the book!"

While I am ashamed, I am unrepentant.

Made in the USA
San Bernardino, CA
13 December 2018